The St. Lawrence Lowlands

Bryan Pezzi

Weigl

CALGARY
www.weigl.ca

Published by Weigl Educational Publishers Limited
6325 – 10 Street SE
Calgary, Alberta, Canada
T2H 2Z9

Web site: www.weigl.ca

Library and Archives Canada Cataloguing in Publication

Pezzi, Bryan
        The St. Lawrence lowlands / Brian Pezzi.
(Canadian geographic regions)
Includes index.
ISBN 1-55388-146-X (bound).--ISBN 1-55388-152-4 (pbk.)
        1. Saint Lawrence River Valley--Geography--Textbooks.
I. Title. II. Series.
FC2756.P49 2005   917.14   C2005-904560-4

                Printed in the United States of America
                1 2 3 4 5 6 7 8 9 0   09 08 07 06 05

COVER: Over a million lakes and rivers dot the St. Lawrence Lowlands.

Cover: Jean du Boisberranger/The Image Bank/Getty Images (front); Konrad Wothe/Science
Faction/Getty Images (back); **European Space Agency:** page 41 (ESA/MERIS); **Getty Images:** pages 3
(Michael Melford/National Geographic), 4L (Steve Bly/The Image Bank), 4ML (Paul Nicklen/National
Geographic), 4MR (Philip & Karen Smith/Stone), 4R (Francesca York/Dorling Kindersley), 5L
(Raymond K. Gehman/National Geographic), 5M (John Dunn/National Geographic), 5R (Ed
Simpson/Stone), 6 (Cosmo Condina/Stone), 11 (Panoramic Images), 13 (Ross Rappaport/Photonica),
14 (MPI), 15 (MPI), 16 (Time Life Pictures/Mansell/Time Life Pictures), 17 (Glen Allison/Stone), 18
(Marty Honig/Photodisc Green), 19 (PhotoLink/Photodisc Red), 21T (Altrendo Panoramic/Altrendo),
21B (Jason Reed/Photodisc Green), 29 (Brian Gomsak), 30 (PhotoLink/Photodisc Green), 31 (Gary
Vestal/Photographer's Choice), 32 (Walter Bibikow/Taxi), 33 (Michael Orton/Photographer's Choice),
35 (Ross Durant/FoodPix), 36 (Konrad Wothe/Science Faction), 37 (Robert Cable/Digital Vision), 38
(Steve Allen/Brand X Pictures), 39 (Brian Skerry/National Geographic), 40 (Jean du
Boisberranger/The Image Bank), 42 (Nancy Simmerman/ Stone), 43TL (Getty Images/Taxi), 43TR
(Nicholas Veasey/Photographer's Choice), 43ML (Tom Schierlitz/The Image Bank), 43MR (Bill
Greenblatt/Liaison), 43BL (Maria Stenzel/National Geographic), 43BR (Bryce Flynn Photography
Inc/Taxi), 44L (Stockdisc/Stockdisc Classic), 44M (Ryan McVay/Photodisc Green), 44R (C Squared
Studios/Photodisc Green), 45L (Tom Schierlitz/The Image Bank), 45R (Stockdisc/Stockdisc Classic);
Photos.com: pages 7, 20, 22, 23, 24, 25, 28, 34.

Substantive Editor
Arlene Worsley

Copy Editors
Frances Purslow
Janice L. Redlin

Designer
Terry Paulhus

Layout
Kathryn Livingstone
Gregg Muller

Photo Researchers
Annalise Bekkering
Jennifer Hurtig

We acknowledge the financial
support of the Government of
Canada through the Book
Publishing Industry Development
Program (BPIDP) for our
publishing activities.

CONTENTS

The Regions of Canada

Canada is the second largest country on Earth. It occupies an enormous area of land on the North American continent. Studying geography helps draw attention to the seven diverse Canadian regions, including their land, climate, vegetation, and wildlife. Learning about geography also helps in understanding the people in each region, their history, and their culture. The word "geography" comes from Greek and means "earth description."

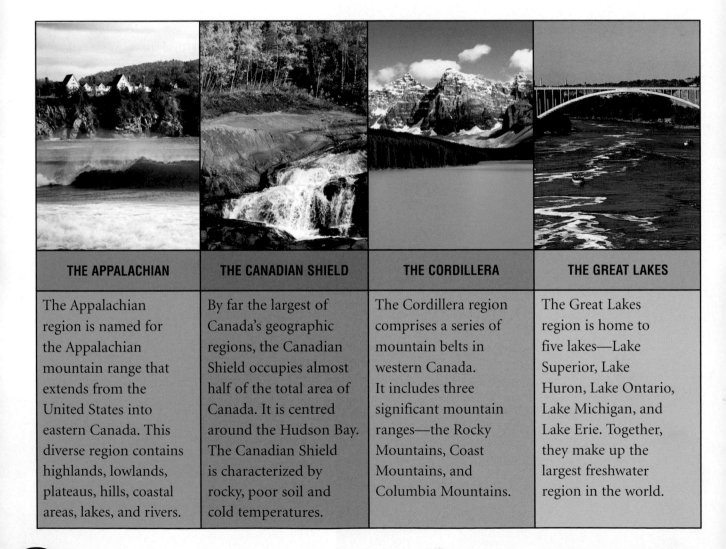

THE APPALACHIAN	THE CANADIAN SHIELD	THE CORDILLERA	THE GREAT LAKES
The Appalachian region is named for the Appalachian mountain range that extends from the United States into eastern Canada. This diverse region contains highlands, lowlands, plateaus, hills, coastal areas, lakes, and rivers.	By far the largest of Canada's geographic regions, the Canadian Shield occupies almost half of the total area of Canada. It is centred around the Hudson Bay. The Canadian Shield is characterized by rocky, poor soil and cold temperatures.	The Cordillera region comprises a series of mountain belts in western Canada. It includes three significant mountain ranges—the Rocky Mountains, Coast Mountains, and Columbia Mountains.	The Great Lakes region is home to five lakes—Lake Superior, Lake Huron, Lake Ontario, Lake Michigan, and Lake Erie. Together, they make up the largest freshwater region in the world.

Canada is home to a variety of landforms. The country hosts sweeping Arctic **tundra**, fertile lowlands, rolling plains, majestic mountains, and vast forests. Each region has a wide range of plants, animals, natural resources, industries, and people.

THE INTERIOR PLAINS	THE NORTH	THE ST. LAWRENCE LOWLANDS
The rolling, low-lying landscape of the Interior Plains is the primary centre for agriculture in Canada. The Interior Plains region lies between the Cordillera and the Canadian Shield.	Much of the North region is composed of thousands of islands north of the Canadian mainland. Distinctive landforms in the region include Arctic lowlands and polar deserts. Glacier mountains are also a recognizable feature in the North.	The St. Lawrence Lowlands region is located on fertile soil surrounding the St. Lawrence River. The region contains a waterway system linking Canada and the United States to the Atlantic Ocean.

A River Runs Through It

The St. Lawrence Lowlands region is sandwiched between two much larger regions: the Canadian Shield to the northwest and the Appalachian to the southeast. The region takes its name from one of Canada's most important rivers, the St. Lawrence. The **lowlands** are a long, narrow area that follows the St. Lawrence River from the eastern tip of Ontario through southern Quebec to the Gulf of St. Lawrence and the Atlantic Ocean.

Located to the southwest of the St. Lawrence Lowlands is another low-lying region called the Great Lakes. Together these lowlands form a system of lakes and waterways that moves water from the inland Great Lakes to the Atlantic Ocean hundreds of kilometres away.

From Brockville to Quebec

The St. Lawrence Lowlands begins near the city of Brockville, Ontario, and extends northeastward to Quebec City, Quebec. In between these two cities can be found many urban areas, including Montreal, the largest city in the region. Ottawa, the

Founded in 1608, Quebec City was the first European settlement in the St. Lawrence Lowlands.

Ottawa, the capital city of Canada, lies on the Rideau Canal. In 2005, Ottawa was 150 years old.

nation's capital, is also located in the St. Lawrence Lowlands. It lies on the Ottawa River, which flows into the St. Lawrence River. Part of the St. Lawrence Lowlands region extends into the United States around Lake Champlain. This long, narrow lake is located just south of Quebec, on the border between Vermont and New York State.

Historically, the St. Lawrence River has played an important role in Canada's exploration and development. The first Europeans to explore Canada travelled this route. It was here that they met the region's First Nations Peoples and learned about a different way of life. Canada's first large settlements were built upon the banks of the St. Lawrence River.

QUICK FACTS

- Montreal had a population of 875,000 people in 1941. Today, the population is more than 3.5 million.

- Trois-Rivières is Canada's second oldest city. It was founded in 1634.

- Ile d'Orléans is an island in the St. Lawrence River, near Quebec City. It is known for its historic homes and churches.

- Ottawa is the capital city of Canada. It is home to the Parliament Buildings, the National Gallery, and the National Archives of Canada.

- The St. Lawrence Lowlands region has a national capital (Ottawa, Ontario), a provincial capital (Quebec City, Quebec), and the second-largest city in the country (Montreal, Quebec).

- Hydro Quebec and Ontario Hydro provide most of the electricity in the St. Lawrence Lowlands. The companies are owned and operated by the governments of Quebec and Ontario, respectively.

- Salaberry-de-Valleyfield is located on the south shore of the St. Lawrence River. Every summer, the town hosts one of North America's biggest speedboat regattas.

Map of Canadian Geographic Regions

This map of Canada shows the seven geographic regions that make up the country. The regions are divided by their **topography**, from towering mountains to river valleys, and from Arctic tundra to rolling prairies. Canadian geographic regions are some of the most diverse anywhere in the world.

Studying a map of Canada's geographic regions helps develop an understanding of them, and about the nation as a whole.

YUKON TERRITORY

Gulf of Alaska

Whitehorse

PACIFIC OCEAN

BRITISH COLUMBIA

Kamloops

Victoria   Vancouver

N
W   E
S

0   500 Kilometres

LEGEND

	The Appalachian
	The Canadian Shield
	The Cordillera
	The Great Lakes
	The Interior Plains
	The North
	The St. Lawrence Lowlands

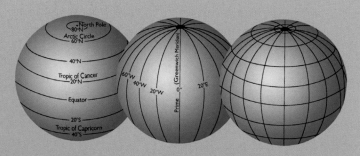

North Pole
80°N
Arctic Circle
60°N
40°N
Tropic of Cancer
20°N
Equator
20°S
Tropic of Capricorn
40°S

60°W 40°W 20°W Prime (Greenwich Meridian) 0° 20°E

Latitude and Longitude

Longitude measures the distance from a spot on the map to an imaginary line called the prime meridian that runs around the globe from the North Pole to the South Pole.

Latitude measures the distance from a spot on the map to an imaginary line called the equator that runs around the middle of the globe.

The Map Scale

A map scale is a type of formula. The scale helps determine how to calculate distances between places on a map.

```
|---------|---------|
0         500 Kilometres
```

The Compass Rose

North is indicated on the map by the compass rose. As well, the cardinal directions—north, south, east, and west—and the intermediate directions—northeast, southeast, northwest, southwest—are shown.

Regions of the World

Earth is always moving and changing. Sometimes these changes happen slowly, over millions of years. Other times, an event such as an earthquake or a volcano eruption can cause sudden, dramatic changes. Whether they occur gradually or suddenly, these changes are responsible for creating different geographic regions.

> "Every continent has a variety of geographic regions. They all have highlands and lowlands, mountains, and deserts."

The Story of Pangaea

The reason Earth has similar regions in different countries is that the world was once made up of one continent, or landmass. In 1912, Alfred Wegener, a German geologist and meteorologist, called this supercontinent Pangaea. He proposed the theory that Pangaea covered nearly half Earth's surface and was surrounded by an ocean called Panthalassa. Between 245 and 208 million years ago,

PERMIAN
225 million years ago

TRIASSIC
200 million years ago

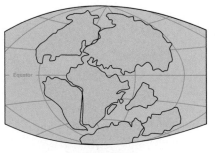

JURASSIC
135 million years ago

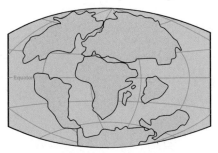

CRETACEOUS
65 million years ago

The Gulf of St. Lawrence is one of the most ancient landforms in the world, having been formed almost 500 million years ago by the partial closing of a prehistoric ocean.

Pangaea began to separate. The pieces of the larger landmass moved apart until they formed seven continents—Africa, Antarctica, Asia, Australia, Europe, North America, and South America.

Regional Variety

Every continent has a variety of geographic regions, including highlands, lowlands, mountains, and deserts. Lowlands have a very low altitude. They are usually found in river valleys, which take water from the interior and move it out to sea. The rivers help provide fertile soil and transportation routes, making lowlands an attractive place for people to live.

One of Earth's earliest centres of urban civilization was that of Ancient Mesopotamia. Thousands of years ago, this culture grew in the lowlands between the Tigris and Euphrates Rivers in Asia. These rivers, located in present-day Iraq and Syria, provided a good region for people to grow food and build cities. Ancient Egypt, another early civilization, grew upon the banks of the Nile River in Africa more than 5,000 years ago. Many of the world's important cities have developed in the lowlands of great rivers. Cairo (Egypt), Shanghai (China), and London (Great Britain) are a few examples.

QUICK FACTS

- The St. Lawrence River is the nineteenth-longest river in the world. The Nile is the longest river.

- The St. Lawrence is the third-longest river in Canada, after the Mackenzie and the Yukon Rivers.

- Fertile lowlands exist elsewhere, too. The Netherlands has lowlands that are below sea level. This land is protected from flooding by dikes.

Glacial Effect on Canada

Canada's geographic regions were formed by the actions of ice thousands of years ago. As ice freezes, melts, and moves over land, it leaves its mark on the terrain below. This process is called **glaciation**, and it is triggered by changes in climate. Scientists believe that Earth has experienced many ice ages. These are periods when Earth's temperature turns colder and giant sheets of ice cover large areas. These large masses of ice are called glaciers. The largest glaciers can be as thick as 4 kilometres deep and cover the entire landscape of a region, except for its highest peaks. Sometimes, they can spread over most of a continent.

> " Scientists call this Ice Age the Wisconsin because it reached all the way from the North Pole to the state of Wisconsin. "

Currently, the world is experiencing an interglacial period, or a period between ice ages. About 18,000 years ago, Canada was almost entirely covered in ice. Scientists call this Ice Age the Wisconsin because it reached all the way from the North Pole to what

The Formation of the Champlain Sea

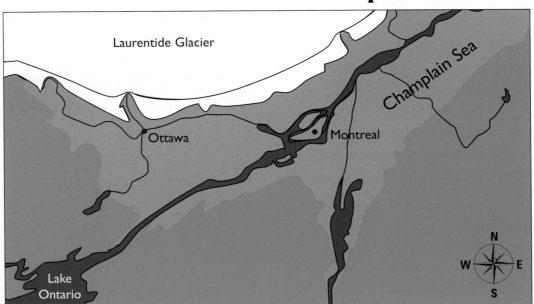

The weight of the Laurentide ice sheet caused the St. Lawrence Lowlands region to sink. The melting glacier filled this area with water, forming the Champlain Sea.

is now the state of Wisconsin. The Wisconsin Ice Age lasted 100,000 years and dramatically altered the land that became Canada.

Ice Forms the Lowlands

During this time, an ice sheet called the Laurentide covered what is now the St. Lawrence Lowlands. Ice sheets do not stay in one place. The weight of a glacier causes it to move over land at an average of 30 centimetres per day—and as much as 30 to 80 metres per day. This movement can create valleys in the land far below. When the Laurentide ice sheet receded, it left a low valley in its place. That is how the St. Lawrence Lowlands was formed.

As the glaciers drained vast amounts of water into the world's oceans, the sea level rose. Water drained into the St. Lawrence and Ottawa Valleys, forming the Champlain Sea. For about 3,000 years, the sea covered the land between Quebec City, Quebec, and Brockville, Ontario. It also extended up the Ottawa River Valley to Pembroke, Ontario.

About 10,000 years ago, the waters of the Champlain Sea receded. Where there once was a great sea, there is now the St. Lawrence River.

Ammonite mollusks are extinct animals that lived in the world's oceans millions of years ago.

WHAT WAS THE CHAMPLAIN SEA?

The St. Lawrence Lowlands was once entirely under water. About 13,000 years ago, water from the Atlantic Ocean flooded the St. Lawrence and Ottawa River Valleys, forming a great inland body of water called the Champlain Sea. At this time, the flat valley floor of the St. Lawrence Lowlands was actually a seabed. The Monteregian Hills, which now look down upon the valley, were islands in the Champlain Sea. Fragments of marine creatures have been found in the sands and clays of the lowlands. These include ancient shell fossils and beluga whale skeletons.

The First Inhabitants

The Europeans were not the first people to explore and settle in the St. Lawrence Lowlands. The region was inhabited for thousands of years before their arrival. The first inhabitants in the St. Lawrence Lowlands were Canada's First Nations Peoples.

The **indigenous** population before European contact consisted of many different cultures. Each had its own language and customs. The **Iroquoian** and **Algonquian** groups lived in the St. Lawrence Lowlands. The climate and rich soil of the lowlands supported their crops of corn, tobacco, and beans. In addition to farming, they also fished and hunted in the forests.

Contact with Europeans

The indigenous peoples of the St. Lawrence Lowlands maintained their way of life for many centuries. Change began to occur upon contact with Europeans. The French came to the St. Lawrence area, first to explore, and later to settle the region. These early interactions between cultures were often peaceful and cooperative. The First Nations Peoples known as the Huron and the Abenaki welcomed the French colonists and helped them survive in the new land. They taught them how to manoeuvre canoes through the rapids of the St. Lawrence River, and how to travel by toboggan and snowshoe. The First Nations Peoples traded furs for European tools, utensils, and weapons.

Although these early interactions provided many benefits, contact with Europeans proved to be destructive to the population of the First Nations. The Europeans exposed the First Nations Peoples to new diseases. The First Nations Peoples also became involved in the fur-trading rivalry

The European fur trade greatly influenced the lives of the Iroquois.

Corn has been an important staple food for First Nations groups in the region.

between the French and the English. The **Iroquois**, allies with English fur traders, became bitter enemies of the French colonists and their First Nations allies. These conflicts made life difficult and dangerous for everyone for many years.

First Nations Today

The descendants of these First Nations Peoples still inhabit the St. Lawrence Lowlands. The Mohawk group live in the area around Montreal. The Montagnais, or Innu, are the largest First Nations group in Quebec. They live in communities along the northern shore of the Gulf of St. Lawrence and in Labrador. Other First Nations communities in the St. Lawrence Lowlands region include the **Algonquins**, Abenakis, and Hurons. Many First Nations Peoples are working to preserve their culture by learning their traditional languages, arts, and spiritual practices.

WHAT FIRST NATIONS PEOPLES LIVE IN THE ST. LAWRENCE LOWLANDS?

First Nations Peoples living in the St. Lawrence lowlands can be divided into two **linguistic** groups, the Algonquian and the Iroquoian.

The Abenaki belong to the Algonquian group. Their community is on the south shore of the St. Lawrence River, near Trois-Rivières. Today there are nearly 2,000 Abenaki in Quebec. The Abenaki have two communities, Odanak and Wolinak.

The Algonquins are also part of the Algonquian family. There are more than 9,000 Algonquins living in western Quebec and northeastern Ontario.

With more than 14,700 people, the Montagnais, or Innu, are the largest First Nations group in Quebec. The Montagnais belong to the Algonquian family.

The Huron-Wendat belong to the Iroquoian linguistic family. The Hurons live on the Wendake reserve north of Quebec City. There are nearly 3,000 Huron in Quebec.

The Mohawk also belong to the Iroquoian group. They have a population of nearly 11,000 in Quebec. The Mohawk community is located near Montreal. The three Mohawk communities in Quebec are Kahnawake, Kanesatake, and Akwesasne.

From Europe to Canada

European sailors crossed the Atlantic Ocean in the 1400s. Italian explorer Christopher Columbus is credited with discovering North America, specifically the United States, in 1492, although Vikings from Iceland and Greenland visited Canada hundreds of years earlier. Columbus' discovery prompted other Europeans to plan voyages to the New World. The goal of many explorers was to find the Northwest Passage—a sea route from North America to Asia. The legendary riches of Asia prompted many hopeful voyages, but the journey was long, difficult, and costly. Often, the journey to find the Northwest Passage ended in North America when explorers discovered all that the land had to offer.

Early explorers of the St. Lawrence Lowlands illustrated their maps with drawings of events and peoples.

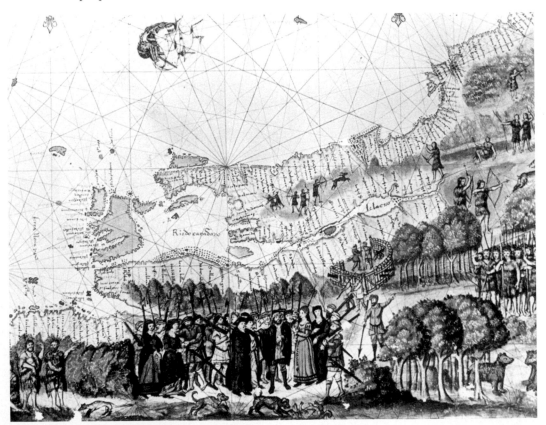

Cartier and Champlain

In 1534, French captain Jacques Cartier sailed to Newfoundland, then turned south toward the Gulf of St. Lawrence. He visited Prince Edward Island and the Gaspé Peninsula, and then discovered the St. Lawrence River.

On his second voyage to the region, Cartier discovered indigenous settlements at Stadacona and Hochelaga, where there was a settlement of over 1,000 Iroquois. The Iroquois led him to the foot of a low mountain, which Cartier named "Mont Réal," meaning Royal Mountain.

Samuel de Champlain's exploration of the St. Lawrence Lowlands helped the French learn about this new land. In 1608, Champlain started a fur-trading post in Quebec City. This was the beginning of a new country, which is why Samuel de Champlain is known as the "father of Canada."

A statue of Samuel de Champlain was contructed in 1898 in Quebec City, honouring one of the most influential explorers of the region.

QUICK FACTS

▶ During the fur trade, beaver pelts were highly valued because they were almost waterproof. The pelts were worn as furs or made into fashionable hats. Fox, mink, marten, and otter furs were also traded.

▶ The name "Canada" comes from the Huron-Iroquois word *kanata*, which means "village" or "settlement." Jacques Cartier used the name Canada to refer to the area around Quebec City.

Lore of the Lowlands

THE DEVIL IN QUEBEC FOLKLORE

French Canadians have a wealth of folk stories that date to the time of the French settlement along the St. Lawrence River. The Devil is in many of these stories and is often portrayed as a trickster who wears disguises and plots devious schemes.

One story tells about how the Devil obtained a cat. The cat lived in a convent near Quebec City. The convent had been built beside a shrine. Pilgrims with illnesses and disabilities would come to visit the shrine from far and wide. Here, they would be healed through the power of God. To get to this holy place, the pilgrims had to cross an old wooden bridge that had been built over a creek. One day the old bridge broke, and all the pilgrims fell into the water. The convent's Mother Superior was very upset and wanted to build a new, stone bridge over the creek.

The Devil saw Mother Superior's problem and decided to play a trick on her. Dressed in disguise, the Devil approached Mother Superior and said he would build her the best bridge she had ever seen. He just had one condition. He would claim the first thing that crossed over the new bridge as his payment. Mother Superior agreed to this condition, and construction started at once.

Once the last stone was put in place, Mother Superior approached the bridge with a large bag in her hand. The Devil thought that she would be the first to cross, and he would claim her soul as his prize. Instead, Mother Superior opened up her bag, and the cat jumped out. It ran across the bridge and leaped onto the Devil's shoulder. The Devil was furious. He screamed and disappeared into a black puff of smoke, taking the cat with him.

AN IROQUOIS LEGEND

The Iroquois of the St. Lawrence Lowlands have a rich heritage of storytelling. In the legend of Thunder Boy, a man, his wife, and their daughter lived alone on an island. During a thunderstorm, a heavy mist surrounded the girl and lifted her up into the sky.

The girl found herself in the land of the Thunder People. One of the men fell in love with her. His father, the chief, told his son he had to return to Earth every day to find food for her.

For 1 year, the girl lived in the country of the Thunder People. One day the chief said, "My daughter, you are to give birth to a son. He cannot be born in this land. You must return to your old home. Once he is born, guard him carefully. If anyone strikes him, you will lose him."

The girl returned to her family and gave birth. Whenever a thunderstorm occurred, the boy ran out in the rain, where he laughed and played. The boy's grandmother did not like that behaviour, so she locked him in their cabin. The boy became angry and smashed their belongings. The old woman lost her temper, grabbed a stick, and gave the boy a sharp blow across his legs. There was a blinding flash of lightning and a roar of thunder. The room filled with heavy mist, and the boy disappeared. When the boy's mother returned, she said, "You struck my son, so his father has taken him to live in the land of the Thunder People."

The Thunder People are friendly toward the Iroquois because the boy is half-Iroquois. According to legend, when thunder first occurs in the spring, throwing tobacco in fire will please the Thunder People.

Flat Plains and Rising Hills

The St. Lawrence Lowlands region lies mainly in the province of Quebec. It is one of three geographic regions in the province. The other two regions are the Canadian Shield and the Appalachian. Each region is distinct because of its diverse topography.

The landforms that make up the St. Lawrence Lowlands consist of low, flat plains and gently rolling hills. Below the surface is a layer of sedimentary rock. Broad terraces gently slope down toward the St. Lawrence River, which dominates this region. The area is made up of three plains named the Quebec Plain, the Trois-Rivières Plain, and the Montreal Plain. These plains are long and narrow, in some places only 1 kilometre wide along the river. The land is low and flat, which is ideal for farming and building highways.

> "The hills start at Montreal and extend eastward toward the Appalachian."

Fertile soil, moderate temperatures, and proximity to water have all helped to make the St. Lawrence Lowlands one of the most productive and populous areas in Quebec.

The St. Lawrence Lowlands are bordered by the Canadian Shield's Laurentian Mountains to the north.

Eight hills named the Monteregian Hills rise suddenly from the lowlands in the St. Lawrence River valley. These hills formed millions of years ago when underground molten rock pushed up through Earth's surface and cooled. The hills are located in Montreal and extend eastward toward the Appalachian region. Some of the Monteregian Hills have apple orchards, while others offer recreational activities such as skiing. The highest of the hills is Mount Brome, which reaches 553 metres above sea level. Mount Royal is 233 metres high and overlooks the city of Montreal.

The Richter scale was invented in 1935. It measures the size of seismic waves from earthquakes.

QUICK FACTS

- The St. Lawrence River has the tenth-largest **drainage basin** in the world.

- In 1663, a severe earthquake hit the St. Lawrence Lowlands. The tremors were so strong that forests, waterfalls, and houses were destroyed. Amazingly, no one was killed or injured.

Journey to the Sea

The St. Lawrence Lowlands connects Canada's most important system of waterways. This complex system starts at the Great Lakes, hundreds of kilometres to the southwest. Water from the Great Lakes flows out of Lake Ontario in southeastern Ontario. It makes its long journey along the St. Lawrence River toward the sea. Along the way, water from other river systems also flows into the St. Lawrence. The Ottawa River is part of this system. It flows through Ottawa and joins the St. Lawrence River near Montreal. Other important river systems that drain into the St. Lawrence include the Richelieu, Saguenay, St. François, and St. Maurice.

Rapids on the River

In some places, the waters of the St. Lawrence flow gently and smoothly. In other areas, natural obstacles make the journey rougher. A 38-metre drop near the border between Ontario and Quebec creates many rapids, including the Lachine Rapids. These rapids, near Montreal, made travelling this part of the river difficult for early explorers. The Lachine Canal was built in 1825 to overcome this problem. It was replaced by the South Shore Canal in 1959.

Many travellers used to carry their boats over land to avoid the rapids on the St. Lawrence River.

Anticosti Island is more than 220 kilometres long and up to 56 kilometres wide.

The St. Lawrence River flows in a northeasterly direction. It begins to widen near Quebec City. Eventually, the river flows into the Gulf of St. Lawrence and the Atlantic Ocean. The Gulf of St. Lawrence is one of the world's largest estuaries. An estuary is a body of water where a river meets the sea. In an estuary, fresh water from the river mixes together with the salt water of the sea. The ocean's tides influence this mixing action. Where the tides are strong, the waters mix and become salty, similar to the ocean. Where the tides are weaker, little mixing occurs, and the water has less salt.

The largest island in the Gulf of St. Lawrence is Anticosti Island. Home to steep limestone cliffs and a huge bog, this island is sparsely populated. Although it is larger than the province of Prince Edward Island, Anticosti Island has about 250 inhabitants.

QUICK FACTS

- Every second, the St. Lawrence River empties about 11,000 cubic metres of water into the Gulf of St. Lawrence.

- The St. Lawrence Lowlands includes small, isolated areas of Quebec's north shore, as well as portions of coastline in Newfoundland and Labrador.

- Estuaries provide a natural location for commercial seaports such as Montreal. London (Great Britain), New York (United States), and Hamburg (Germany) are all important centres of commerce that have developed on estuaries.

Four Seasons

Nearly all the people in Canada live in the southern part of the country, near the border with the United States. The southern climate is warmer and more hospitable than the harsh, frozen north. The weather in the St. Lawrence Lowlands is moderate. The area has four distinct seasons, each with its own character.

Air Masses Make the Weather

The weather patterns of the St. Lawrence Lowlands are strongly affected by large air masses from other North American areas. A weather system in the Canadian Arctic or the Gulf of Mexico can affect Ottawa or Quebec City. Arctic air masses moving southward bring cold, stormy weather. Warm, moist air from the Gulf of Mexico provides most of the moisture for the region, making summers warm and humid. Thunderstorms are common in the summer, while snowstorms often occur in the winter months. When the temperature in the St. Lawrence Lowlands rises above 0° Celsius, usually in March, spring has arrived. In July, the

"The St. Lawrence Lowlands has four distinct seasons, each with its own character."

The downward-sloping branches of coniferous trees allow heavy snow to slide off without breaking branches.

The St. Lawrence Lowlands' forests contain a mixture of deciduous and coniferous trees.

average daily temperature is 21° Celsius. Sometimes, temperatures can exceed 30° Celsius, although readings that high are rare in this region.

Autumn arrives in late September, when average daily temperatures fall below 16° Celsius. As the season progresses, days become shorter and colder, and the leaves of trees and shrubs turn shades of gold, orange, and bright red.

The Arrival of Winter

Winter usually arrives in November, when average daily temperatures fall below 0° Celsius. Winter can last for more than 4 months. Montreal receives about 230 centimetres of snow every winter, and Quebec City more than 300 centimetres. Intense storms can move in from the central United States or from the Atlantic coast.

QUICK FACTS

- Ice storms are an especially hazardous form of weather. In an ice storm, freezing rain forms a layer of ice on roads, making automobile travel nearly impossible.

- In the past, the St. Lawrence River was used as a transportation and communication route. The river was often frozen from December until April, which made it difficult for ships to pass through.

Charting the Climate

A region's climate can indicate what it is like to live there. Temperature, snowfall, and even growing seasons are all part of climate.

Information is collected when studying a region's climate. The maps and charts on these pages help describe this information in a visual way.

Average Temperature

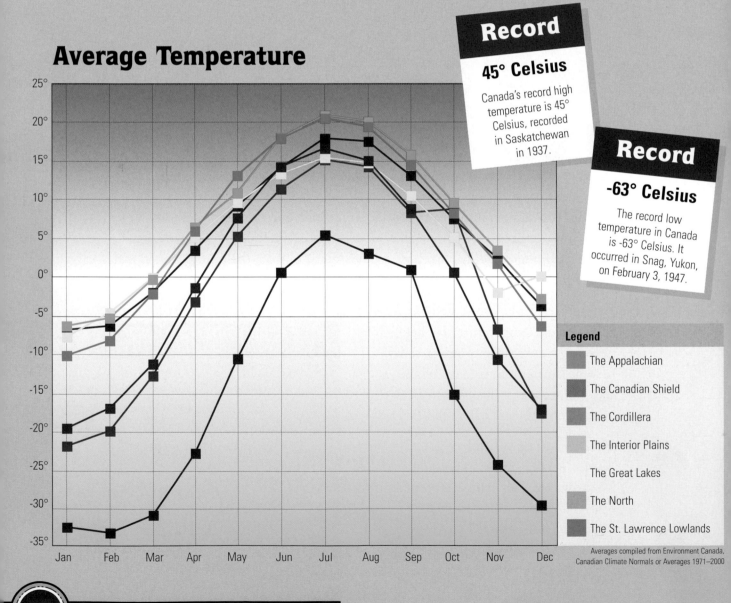

Record

45° Celsius

Canada's record high temperature is 45° Celsius, recorded in Saskatchewan in 1937.

Record

-63° Celsius

The record low temperature in Canada is -63° Celsius. It occurred in Snag, Yukon, on February 3, 1947.

Legend
- The Appalachian
- The Canadian Shield
- The Cordillera
- The Interior Plains
- The Great Lakes
- The North
- The St. Lawrence Lowlands

Averages compiled from Environment Canada, Canadian Climate Normals or Averages 1971–2000

Average Snowfall

Legend
- over 400 cm
- 300 - 400 cm
- 200 - 300 cm
- 100 - 200 cm
- under 100 cm

Source: Canadian Oxford World Atlas, 4th Edition, 1998

Record

118.1 cm

The record 1-day snowfall, on January 17, 1974, was 118.1 centimetres at Lakelse Lake, British Columbia.

Growing Season

Legend

Average number of days with a median temperature over 5° C
- under 60
- 60 - 100
- 100 - 140
- 140 - 180
- 180 - 220
- 220 - 260
- over 260

Source: Canadian Oxford World Atlas, 4th Edition, 1998

The 1998 Ice Storm

An ice storm is one of the most dangerous winter storms. This weather condition occurs when freezing rain hits the ground and turns to ice. Ice storms do not take place very often, but when they do there can be much damage.

The ice storm of 1998 was one of the most serious natural disasters in Canada's history. It was caused by El Niño, a weather phenomenon that starts in the Pacific Ocean near South America and affects weather patterns all over the world. In 1998, a huge, warm, wet air mass from the Gulf of Mexico collided with heavy, cold air from the Arctic. Raindrops formed in the warm layer of air, fell, and cooled as they hit colder air near the ground. This freezing rain turned into a layer of ice that covered streets, trees, and electric utility wires.

One-quarter of Quebeckers sought refuge. After a week, the freezing rain ended, but the weather turned colder.

Widespread Damage

The ice storm affected a large area. From Ontario to the Maritimes, the storm caused damage and devastation. Montreal, Quebec, was very hard hit. On the morning of January 5, Montrealers woke up to find their city covered with ice. Throughout the city, millions of trees fell under the weight of the ice. As well, thousands of utility poles fell, including 130 transmission towers, 1,000 steel electrical pylons, and 25,000 wooden transmission poles. Blackouts occurred throughout the Montreal area, leaving buildings with no light or heat. Electricity did not work in 700,000 homes.

Nearly 100,000 people had to abandon their homes to the frigid cold for the duration of the 1998 ice storm.

The 1998 ice storm made roads dangerous or even inaccessible to nearly 2.6 million people.

Recovery Begins

The ice storm lasted many days. By the fourth day, a state of emergency was declared in Quebec. The Canadian Armed Forces set up emergency shelters and delivered supplies. One-quarter of Quebeckers sought refuge. After a week, the freezing rain ended, but the weather turned much colder. After 2 weeks, power returned to parts of Montreal. However, some areas were without electricity for as long as 33 days.

At least thirty-five people—twenty-two in Quebec and thirteen elsewhere—died because of the ice storm. About 25 percent of Montreal's trees were lost, and the province's maple syrup industry suffered serious damage. In total, the storm caused $3 billion in damages, making it Canada's most expensive natural disaster ever.

HOW DID PEOPLE SURVIVE THE ICE STORM?

The ice storm of 1998 became an exercise in survival for the 2 million people trapped on the island of Montreal. The ordinary tasks of everyday life became challenging. Roads were blocked by fallen trees and electricity poles. Subway lines could not run because there was no power. Transportation on the island was nearly impossible. At home, many people had to live without light or heat. Some Montrealers relied on gas and wood stoves. Without essential utilities, life at home was similar to a camping trip. People played board games or read by candlelight to pass the time. Some people had to seek refuge in one of the hundreds of shelters around the city. Other people took shelter wherever there was power and space—office buildings, shopping malls, and even hockey arenas.

Water Works

The St. Lawrence Lowlands is a wealthy industrial region that includes one-sixth of Canada's population. Hydroelectrical power, manufacturing, and logging provide many jobs. These industries rely on raw materials from other regions, which are then transported and processed around the St. Lawrence River.

Lumber is Big Business in a Land with Few Trees

Forest resources are a major industry in the St. Lawrence Lowlands, even though there are few dense forests left in the region. Most forests were cleared many years ago so that land could be used for farms and towns. Lumber is transported along the St. Lawrence River from other regions in Canada. It is taken to sawmills or papermaking plants. Trois-Rivières is a central place for the pulp and paper industry. Much of Canada's newsprint is produced in Trois-Rivières.

> " In 1954, Canada and the United States started work on a project called the St. Lawrence Seaway, to open the river to traffic from the sea. "

The St. Lawrence River provides energy in the form of **hydropower**. Fifteen power plants border the St. Lawrence River in Quebec. The river also provides a means of shipping products to and from the region. Montreal and Quebec City have large ports. These ports act as Canada's gateway to the Atlantic Ocean, providing the shortest distance to Europe of all the primary ports in North America. The river's

Chains of logs are attached across a section of water to keep timber floating down river from drifting.

port system handles more than 11 million tonnes of cargo each year.

The St. Lawrence Seaway

Many years ago, people in both Canada and the United States recognized the importance of the St. Lawrence River for transporting goods. At the time, large sea vessels had difficulty travelling many parts of the river. In 1954, Canada and the United States started work on a project called the St. Lawrence Seaway, to open the river to traffic from the sea. This complex inland water transportation system opened in 1959. Dams, locks, channels, and dikes were built so that large ships could travel easily between the Great Lakes and the Gulf of St. Lawrence. Today, the St. Lawrence Seaway is open from early April to mid-December. Ships on the seaway carry mostly heavy raw materials. It takes a ship 8 to 10 days to sail from Lake Superior to the Atlantic Ocean.

Many people are employed in shipping and goods manufacturing, as well as the region's service industry. Recreation and tourism in the St. Lawrence Lowlands generates more than $3 billion dollars annually.

QUICK FACTS

- The Biosphere is a major tourist attraction in Montreal. This interactive, educational centre teaches visitors about the **ecosystems** of the Great Lakes and St. Lawrence waters.

- Building the St. Lawrence Seaway was a major effort. Its construction involved moving 192.5 million cubic metres of earth, adding 5.7 cubic metres of concrete, building 72 kilometres of dikes, and digging 110 kilomtres of channels.

Rich and Fertile

The St. Lawrence Lowlands region is the second highest producing agricultural region in Canada, next to the Interior Plains. Soil is very rich and productive because the St. Lawrence Lowlands was once flooded by the sea for a long period of time. Organisms and plants fell into the sea, leaving multiple layers of sediment behind. This sediment provides very fertile soil. The sea floor also created flat land, making conditions good for the development of agricultural land.

Most of Quebec's agriculture can be found in the low-lying plains along the St. Lawrence River. Long before Europeans arrived, the indigenous people grew vegetable crops to feed their communities. When the first Europeans arrived in the sixteenth century, they built their first settlements on this rich farming land.

Feeding the French

As the first villages and towns were built upon the banks of the St. Lawrence River, farms became necessary to feed the French colonists. The French government encouraged its citizens to move to the area by giving people farmland in the New World. A special system of land division, called the **seigneurial system,** was set up along the St. Lawrence River. The French king gave blocks of land along the river to

Unlike many types of crops found in Canada, corn is native to both North and South America.

Over two-thirds of Canada's dairy production comes from farms in Ontario and Quebec.

the **seigneurs**, or French lords. Each seigneur divided his land into long, narrow strips, which were rented to farmers. The first row of farms along the river was the best land because it had easy access to water and transportation. The seigneur's family usually lived in a house in the middle of the land. The seigneur often built a school, a mill, and a church nearby.

Family Farms Divided

The seigneurial system of land ownership began in the early 1600s and lasted for about 250 years. The farms did well because the land was flat and summer temperatures were good for growing crops. Farms supplied food for the growing towns and cities along the St. Lawrence River. When a farmer died, his land was usually divided between his children. This resulted in even smaller, narrower farms. The Canadian government officially abolished the seigneurial system in 1854, although many farms along the St. Lawrence still have the long, narrow shape of the original seigneurial farms.

Commercial Farming

Commercial farms provide food for the larger urban centres of the region. Major crops include hay and fodder, grain and corn, barley, soybeans, and oats. Farmers raise livestock such as cattle, sheep, and hogs. Some farmers also raise poultry.

Quebec's dairy farmers supply nearly half of Canada's milk products, including high quality cheeses.

QUICK FACTS

▸ The average size of a farm in Quebec is 96 hectares.

▸ Oka cheese is a smooth, creamy cheese with a butter flavour. It is produced in the St. Lawrence Lowlands.

Wild Wetlands and Maple Forests

The St. Lawrence Lowlands supports a variety of natural habitats. Ecological conditions differ widely in various parts of the region, producing many species of plant life, or "flora." Often, plants are able to survive the winter because their buds are buried in the ground or are close to the surface.

Wetlands Help the Environment

The St. Lawrence River **wetlands** are especially important to the environment. Many plant and animal species thrive because wetlands provide water and nutrients that support life. Plants and bacteria play an important role in filtering water by absorbing nutrients and pollution from the water and then releasing oxygen into the environment.

66 Hardwood trees are also known as deciduous trees. These trees lose their leaves in the autumn and grow new leaves from buds in the spring. 99

Many of the forests that once filled the St. Lawrence Lowlands have been cleared for agriculture and urban development. Gradually, unused farmland is being reforested.

Forests in the Lowlands

Forests also play an important part in the St. Lawrence Lowlands ecosystem. Although much of the region's original woodland was cleared to make room for urban development and agriculture, some original forests still stand. The St. Lawrence Lowlands forest region, extending from the Ottawa Valley to Lac St. Jean and the Appalachian region, has hot, humid summers and cool winters. The region is dominated by hardwood forest. Hardwood trees are also known as deciduous trees. These trees lose their leaves in the autumn and grow new leaves in the spring.

The Magnificent Maple

The most common and well-known tree in this region is the maple. There are different kinds of maple, including the sugar, red, silver, and black maples. These species all grow in the St. Lawrence Lowlands. Maples are valuable for their hard, durable wood, although most people know the maple for its sugar and syrup. The maple leaf is recognized throughout the world as a symbol of Canada. In 1965, Canada adopted its current maple leaf design for the Canadian flag.

WHERE DOES MAPLE SYRUP COME FROM?

Canada is the world's leading producer of maple sugar products. Maple sugar comes from the syrup of the sugar maple, red maple, silver maple, and black maple trees. First Nations Peoples from the St. Lawrence Lowlands and Great Lakes regions enjoyed the sweet sap of the maple tree long before Europeans arrived. When the French settled in the area, the First Nations Peoples demonstrated how to tap maple trees and boil down the sap. Today, Canada produces about 85 percent of the world's maple syrup. There are more than 10,000 maple syrup producers in the country, mostly in Quebec.

Animal Life

The St. Lawrence Lowlands has a variety of habitats for animal species. The area is home to numerous bird species and **freshwater fish** species, as well as other sea animals.

For the Birds

The province of Quebec is home to hundreds of bird species, and many of them nest in the wetlands in or near the St. Lawrence Lowlands. Each spring, birds migrate to the region. Birdwatchers travel to Cap Tourmente National Wildlife Area to view the migration. Also, large colonies of birds make their homes on islands in the estuary.

Life in the Water

The river, the estuary, and the Gulf of St. Lawrence are home to many species of fish, crustaceans, and marine mammals. This region provides a habitat to both freshwater and saltwater fish. Freshwater fish species found in the area include carp, bass, sturgeon, pike, and eel. Saltwater fish include cod, halibut, salmon, and mackerel. Aquatic animals, such as clams, crabs, urchins, and mussels, also live in the region.

The great blue heron is one of the St. Lawrence Lowlands' most distinctive birds.

Several marine mammals, including varieties of whales, seals, and porpoises, live in the Gulf of St. Lawrence and the St. Lawrence estuary. Sometimes, seals and whales move farther inland and take refuge in the St. Lawrence and Saguenay Rivers.

Land Animals

The St. Lawrence Lowlands teems with life on land. There are reptiles such as turtles and snakes, and amphibians such as newts, salamanders, mudpuppies, and frogs. They make their home in the wetlands and low-lying plains next to the St. Lawrence River. Land mammals, including minks, muskrats, beavers, and raccoons, inhabit the areas near freshwater lakes and rivers. As with many other animals of the region, these mammals prefer the shelter of wetland areas.

Zebra Mussels Invade

While most animal species improve the natural environment of the region, some cause problems. Zebra mussels are small mollusks that come from the Black Sea and the Caspian Sea on ships. They reproduce quickly and live in large colonies, and are troublesome in the areas of the St. Lawrence River around Montreal and Quebec City. Zebra mussels eat the plankton that fish need to survive, and they carry diseases, block water flow, and grow on boats and beaches.

The red-spotted newt is still common in the region, but the loss of habitat to industry and agriculture is a constant threat to its survival.

QUICK FACTS

- The sea lamprey is a fish that lives in the Great Lakes and St. Lawrence River. It is a **parasite** that attaches itself to other animals and sucks out their blood. Sea lampreys can be damaging to the ecosystem because they kill many other fish.

- The Atlantic puffin is a common bird in the Gulf of St. Lawrence. Also known as the sea parrot, this species uses its wings to propel itself underwater. Puffins can dive hundreds of metres to catch fish.

Man Versus Nature

Although small in size, the St. Lawrence Lowlands is the most heavily populated and developed region in Canada. Millions of people live close to the St. Lawrence River. As well, there are thousands of businesses, factories, and industrial plants. Human activities cause pollution and damage the environment. Urban areas create garbage, air pollution, and industrial waste. One of the greatest environmental hazards of the region is pollution to the St. Lawrence River system itself. When these problems are not attended to, they can harm plants and animals.

" The beluga whale is threatened by pollution and human activity. "

The Beluga Struggles to Survive

One of the biggest animals of the St. Lawrence ecosystem is the beluga whale. St. Lawrence belugas can be found in the Gulf of St. Lawrence and in the estuary. Many of these whales are spotted near Battures aux Loups Marin, about 100 kilometres downstream from Quebec City. The whales are easily recognizable by their pure, white skin and bulging foreheads.

Though pollution is still a major problem, efforts to control the problem have seen some success.

The beluga whale is threatened by pollution and human activity. Before 1885, there were as many as 50,000 beluga whales in the St. Lawrence River system. Today, scientists believe there are between 500 and 1,000 remaining. Experts think this decline is probably due to high pollution levels in the St. Lawrence River. High levels of mercury, lead, pesticides, and other chemicals are harmful to the animals' health. These chemicals are a result of industrial activity and shipping. Scientists and the government are working together to try to save the St. Lawrence beluga whales. By studying the whales and creating laws to protect them, environmentalists hope to boost beluga numbers in the river system once again.

Q Should we restrict industrial activity in the St. Lawrence Seaway in order to protect the beluga whale?	
NO	**YES**
Much has been done already to protect the beluga. The law prohibits whale hunting, and industry is working hard to operate more cleanly.	Not enough has been done to protect the beluga. Whales are still becoming sick and dying from pollution. We need tougher laws to fight industries that pollute.
Restricting industry might mean that companies will find running their businesses in the region too difficult or too expensive. If businesses shut down, many people will lose their jobs.	If beluga populations increase, it could boost ecotourism in the region. Whale-watching tours could create new jobs and opportunities for local people.
We do not need laws to make industry stop polluting. Business and government can work together to protect the environment. This approach would help the environment without harming industry.	Industry only acts in its own self-interest. The government must force businesses to be environmentally friendly or else nothing will ever change.

View from Above

There are different ways to view a region. Maps and photos, including those from satellites, help to show the region in different ways.

A map is a diagram that shows an area's surface. Maps can demonstrate many details, such as lakes, rivers, borders, towns, and even roads.

Photos can demonstrate what a region looks like close up. In a photo, specific objects, such as buildings, people, and animals, can be seen.

Satellite photos are pictures taken from space. A satellite thousands of metres in the air can show details as small as a car.

Questions:

What information can be obtained from a photo?

How might a map be useful?

What details are indicated on a satellite photo that cannot be seen on a map?

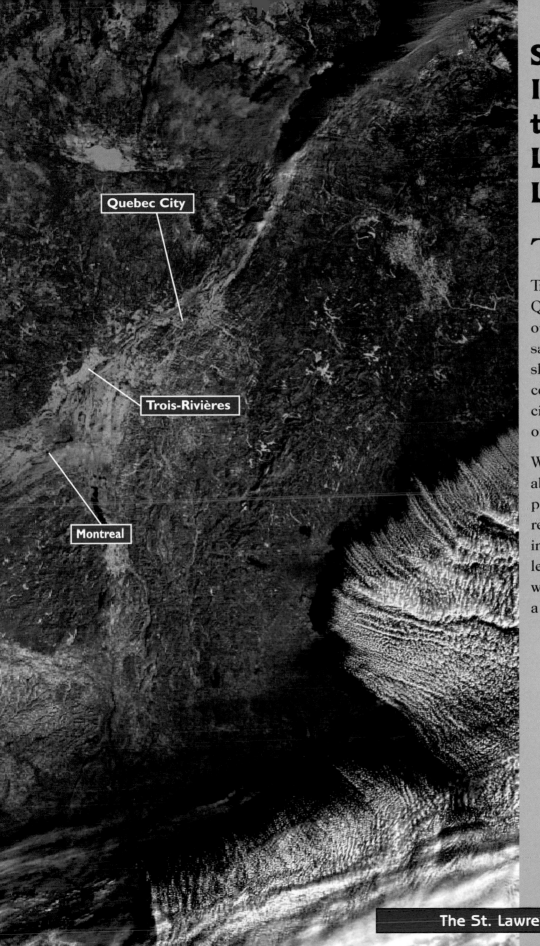

Quebec City

Trois-Rivières

Montreal

Satellite Image of the St. Lawrence Lowlands

The cities of Montreal, Trois-Rivières, and Quebec City stand out clearly on the satellite image. They are shown as a white-grey colour. Surrounding the cities is a large landmass of green vegetation.

What do you notice about this satellite photo compared to a regular photo? What information can you learn from it that you would not learn from a map?

Technology Tools

People have studied geology for hundreds of years. Geologists study the rocks, earth, and surfaces that make up Earth. Even before the science of geology had a name, ancient peoples studied the rocks and minerals around them. They experimented to find out what kind of rocks were used to make weapons, jewellery, and items they needed in daily life. Flint, a type of rock that is easy to shape and sharpen, was used to make spears. Minerals, such as gold and copper, were too soft to use as weapons or tools and were shaped to make beautiful jewellery.

Today, geologists use some tools that have been around for centuries, as well as more modern tools. These tools range from simple pick hammers to sophisticated computer equipment. Geologists use these tools to study the rocks and minerals they find on land. They study geology in other areas, as well. Modern technology and tools help them study geology under the sea, in volcanoes, and even on the Moon.

Careers in Geology

What is a paleontologist?

Answer: A paleontologist studies the history of life on earth. Paleontologists use fossils to learn about prehistoric plants and animals that no longer exist.

Paleontologists need a good understanding of physics, chemistry, biology, and geology to piece together the clues of the ancient past.

Tools of the Trade

Rock hammer or pick:

These special hammers have a flat end that is used to crush larger pieces of rock, and a pointed end, which is used to pick away smaller pieces of rock.

X rays:
X rays help geologists study material in detail. Certain crystals or minerals can be examined very closely by an X ray. Geologists studying ancient fossils or artifacts also use X rays so they can examine delicate objects without damaging them.

Compass:

A compass helps geologists tell which direction they are going. Compasses are very important to geologists, who often work from maps to travel to the areas they are studying.

Seismograph:
A seismograph measures Earth's vibrations. Geologists use seismographs to study the movements of Earth's tectonic plates. Tectonic plates are huge slabs of rock that shift and move beneath Earth's surface. When two or more plates collide, there is an earthquake.

Brushes:
Some of the rocks and materials geologists study are very delicate. Once geologists have uncovered an object in the rock or soil, they use soft brushes to remove dust and debris without causing damage.

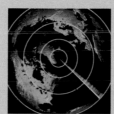

Sonar:
Sonar helps geologists map areas that cannot be reached by humans or seen by the human eye. Sonar sends out a beam of sound. Geologists determine what the sonar has hit by the type of vibration that returns. They can map these locations by listening to the sound.

What is an exploration geologist?

Answer: An exploration geologist uses sophisticated equipment, physics, chemistry, computer modelling, and field mapping techniques to find new mineral resources. Exploration geologists create maps and take samples in the field to study in laboratories.

Where in the World

The St. Lawrence Lowlands lies almost entirely in the province of Quebec. Most of Quebec's population lives in this region. However, there are two other geographic regions in the province as well: the Canadian Shield and the Appalachian.

Look at the list of Quebec cities and towns below. Then, decide in which of the three regions each place belongs. Use a map of the Canadian regions and the information in this book to help you.

Canadian Regions:

The St. Lawrence Lowlands

The Canadian Shield

The Appalachian

Cities and Towns:

Rimouski

Montreal

Matane

Inukjuak

Sept-Îles

Trois-Rivières

Quebec City

Chibougamau

Hull

Gaspé

Port-Menier
(Anticosti Island)

Answers:

St. Lawrence Lowlands: Montreal, Trois-Rivières, Quebec City, Hull, Port-Menier

Canadian Shield: Inukjuak, Sept-Îles, Chibougamau

Appalachian: Rimouski, Matane, Gaspé

Chart Your Course

Imagine you are the captain of a ship hauling cargo through the Great Lakes and the St. Lawrence Seaway. It is your job to transport your cargo from Chicago, Illinois, to Halifax, Nova Scotia. Using a map of North America, trace a path along your route.

Answer the following questions:

1. Which lakes, rivers, oceans, and other bodies of water must you pass through on your journey?

2. How many American states and Canadian provinces must you pass through?

3. Along the way, you must stop five times to refuel. Decide at which ports you want to stop. Using the Internet or your school library, research each of these port cities. Write a paragraph on the importance of these ports to their local economies.

Further Research

Books

Find out more about the St. Lawrence River.

Jenkins, Phil. *River Song: Sailing the History of the St. Lawrence.* Toronto, ON: Penguin Canada, 2001.

Learn more about the ice storm that affected the St. Lawrence Lowlands region.

Abley, Mark. *Stories from the Ice Storm.* Toronto, ON: McClelland & Stewart, 2000.

Web Sites

To learn more about the St. Lawrence Lowlands region, its people, and the provinces that are in it, visit:

The Canadian Encyclopedia Online
www.thecanadianencyclopedia.com

To learn more about Canada and its regions, visit:

Natural Resources Canada
http://atlas.gc.ca/site/english/index.html

Glossary

Algonquian: a linguistic family of some First Nations groups

Algonquins: one group of First Nation Peoples

drainage basin: an area that is drained by a river and its tributaries

ecosystems: all of the living things and nonliving things in specific areas

freshwater fish: fish that inhabit lakes and rivers

glaciation: the action of covering land with ice

hydropower: electricity generated from bodies of water

indigenous: originating and living naturally in an area or environment

Iroquoian: a linguistic family of some First Nations groups

Iroquois: one group of First Nation Peoples

linguistic: having to do with the study of language

lowlands: landforms that lie low on the land, such as plains and wetlands

parasite: a plant or animal that lives with, in, or on another plant or animal for benefit

seigneurial system: a structured French landholding where the state granted parcels of land to seigneurs, who were responsible for securing habitants

seigneurs: persons of rank, especially feudal lords in the ancient regime

topography: detailed description of a land or region

tundra: flat, level, treeless plain

wetlands: a lowland area that is saturated with moisture

Index

CONTENTS

The Regions of Canada

Canada is the second largest country on Earth. It occupies an enormous area of land on the North American continent. Studying geography helps draw attention to the seven diverse Canadian regions, including their land, climate, vegetation, and wildlife. Learning about geography also helps in understanding the people in each region, their history, and their culture. The word "geography" comes from Greek and means "earth description."

THE APPALACHIAN	THE CANADIAN SHIELD	THE CORDILLERA	THE GREAT LAKES
The Appalachian region is named for the Appalachian mountain range that extends from the United States into eastern Canada. This diverse region contains highlands, lowlands, plateaus, hills, coastal areas, lakes, and rivers.	By far the largest of Canada's geographic regions, the Canadian Shield occupies almost half of the total area of Canada. It is centred around the Hudson Bay. The Canadian Shield is characterized by rocky, poor soil and cold temperatures.	The Cordillera region comprises a series of mountain belts in western Canada. It includes three significant mountain ranges—the Rocky Mountains, Coast Mountains, and Columbia Mountains.	The Great Lakes region is home to five lakes—Lake Superior, Lake Huron, Lake Ontario, Lake Michigan, and Lake Erie. Together, they make up the largest freshwater region in the world.

Canada is home to a variety of landforms. The country hosts sweeping Arctic **tundra**, fertile lowlands, rolling plains, majestic mountains, and vast forests. Each region has a wide range of plants, animals, natural resources, industries, and people.

THE INTERIOR PLAINS	THE NORTH	THE ST. LAWRENCE LOWLANDS
The rolling, low-lying landscape of the Interior Plains is the primary centre for agriculture in Canada. The Interior Plains region lies between the Cordillera and the Canadian Shield.	Much of the North region is composed of thousands of islands north of the Canadian mainland. Distinctive landforms in the region include Arctic lowlands and polar deserts. Glacier mountains are also a recognizable feature in the North.	The St. Lawrence Lowlands region is located on fertile soil surrounding the St. Lawrence River. The region contains a waterway system linking Canada and the United States to the Atlantic Ocean.

The Secluded North

The Canadian North is one of the world's most isolated areas. This region covers parts of mainland Northwest Territories and Nunavut, as well as most of the Arctic islands. It is sparsely populated, and access to the area is often difficult. Many of the people who live in the region are Inuit.

The Arctic islands are grouped within Canada's Arctic **Archipelago,** lying north of Canada's mainland. It is the largest group of islands in the world, consisting of more than twenty separate islands and occupying about 1.3 million square kilometres.

> 66 The Arctic islands are the largest group of islands in the world. 99

The North is often regarded as an ice-covered barren terrain—a land of igloos and untouched wilderness. In fact, the North features Canada's second largest mountain range, a variety of wildlife, marine animals, desert land, and vegetation.

The largest islands in the region are Ellesmere Island, Baffin Island, and Victoria Island. Only portions of Ellesmere Island and Baffin Island are considered parts of the Canadian North, while Victoria Island lies entirely within its geographical borders. These are also some of the largest islands in the world.

The Arctic tern nests on rocky islets or sandy beaches. These birds nest in small groups or large colonies of dozens of pairs.

Polar bears thrive in the Arctic. Their dense fur traps in warmth, and a thick layer of fat insulates the bears from the bitter cold.

Axel Heiberg Island, Prince of Wales Island, and Banks Island are some of the smaller islands found in the region.

Significant bodies of water also surround the Arctic islands, including the Arctic Ocean to the north, Beaufort Sea to the west of Banks Island, and Hudson Bay to the south. Waterway systems and bays such as McClure Strait, Viscount Melville Sound, and Lancaster Sound are also found in the North.

QUICK FACTS

▷ The Arctic tern spends the summer in the Arctic and the winter in Antarctica. In a single year, a tern may fly 50,000 kilometres.

▷ There are almost seventy different kinds of fish living in the Arctic waters. The northern pike and lake trout are two of the fish found there.

▷ Days and nights are 6 months long at the North Pole. The summer **solstice** on June 21 is the longest day of the year in the North. Within the Arctic Circle, the Sun does not set on June 21. It will dip toward the horizon at midnight and then continue on its 24-hour journey.

Map of Canadian Geographic Regions

This map of Canada shows the seven geographic regions that make up the country. The regions are divided by their topography, from towering mountains to river valleys, and from Arctic tundra to rolling prairies. Canadian geographic regions are some of the most diverse anywhere in the world.

Studying a map of Canada's geographic regions helps develop an understanding of them, and about the nation as a whole.

LEGEND

- The Appalachian
- The Canadian Shield
- The Cordillera
- The Great Lakes
- The Interior Plains
- The North
- The St. Lawrence Lowlands

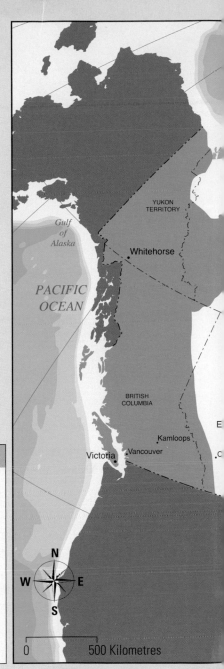

YUKON TERRITORY

Gulf of Alaska

Whitehorse

PACIFIC OCEAN

BRITISH COLUMBIA

Kamloops

Victoria   Vancouver

N
W   E
S

0   500 Kilometres

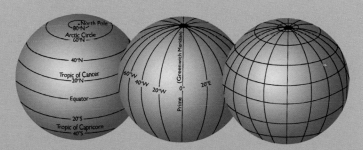

Latitude and Longitude

Longitude measures the distance from a spot on the map to an imaginary line called the prime meridian that runs around the globe from the North Pole to the South Pole.

Latitude measures the distance from a spot on the map to an imaginary line called the equator that runs around the middle of the globe.

The Map Scale

A map scale is a type of formula. The scale helps determine how to calculate distances between places on a map.

0 |————————| 500 Kilometres

The Compass Rose

North is indicated on the map by the compass rose. As well, the cardinal directions—north, south, east, and west—and the intermediate directions—northeast, southeast, northwest, southwest—are shown.

N
W E
S

Earth's Shared History

While the North has many distinct geographical features, some scientists have concluded that the geographic histories of all the various regions of the world share a number of common characteristics.

The Story of Pangaea

The reason Earth has similar regions in different countries is that the world was once made up of one continent. In 1912, Alfred Wegener, a German geologist and meteorologist, called this landmass Pangaea. He proposed the theory that Pangaea covered nearly half of Earth's surface and was surrounded by an ocean called Panthalassa. Between 245 and 208 million years ago, Pangaea began to split. The pieces of the larger landmass moved apart until they formed seven continents—Africa, Antarctica, Asia, Australia, Europe, North America, and South America.

PERMIAN
225 million years ago

TRIASSIC
200 million years ago

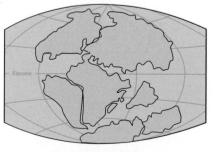

JURASSIC
135 million years ago

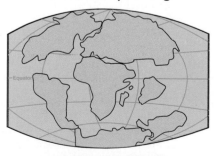

CRETACEOUS
65 million years ago

Tree growth is limited in the Arctic tundra because the land is permanently frozen 25 to 100 centimetres beneath the surface. Only low-lying plants and mosses can survive in this barren soil.

In the North, scientists have found fossilized forests on Axel Heiberg Island that show the region had a much warmer climate 45 million years ago. This supports Wegener's theory of **continental drift**.

The North also shares certain characteristics with other places on Earth. The region's land includes a tundra **biome**, which is found in many regions of the world, including Siberia. The tundra biome is the coldest of the biomes, and is separated into two types—Arctic tundra and alpine tundra. The Arctic tundra in the North is particularly noted for its frost-moulded landscapes, extremely low temperatures, little precipitation, and poor soil nutrients.

QUICK FACTS

- The Arctic tundra is the world's youngest biome. It was formed 10,000 years ago.

- The word "tundra" is from a Finnish word *tunturia*, meaning "treeless plain."

Millions of Years Ago

Over millions of years, the climate of the North has experienced many changes. Its temperatures were both colder and warmer in the past. These differences occurred because of continental drift and the last **Ice Age**.

Glaciers Weigh Down the Land

About 2 million years ago, the North turned cold and snowy with the start of the Pleistocene epoch, or the last Ice Age. Glaciers moved over the land and eventually spread southward, covering most of North America.

> **"** The ice was so heavy that it pushed the land down in places. **"**

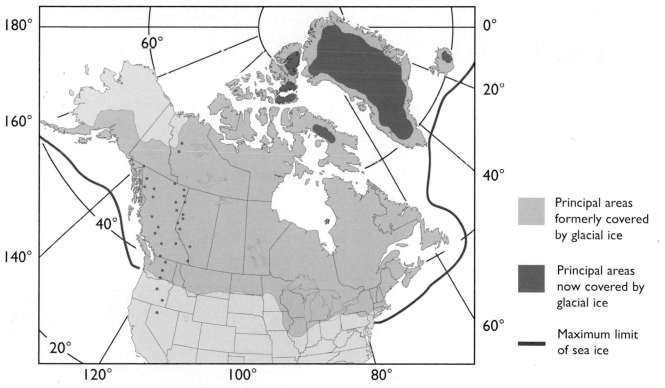

Ice Boundaries

Principal areas formerly covered by glacial ice

Principal areas now covered by glacial ice

Maximum limit of sea ice

During the last Ice Age, about 97 percent of Canada was covered in glacial ice. Today, the areas covered in glacial ice lie in the Cordillera and North.

The weight of all this glacial ice had a tremendous impact on the land. The ice was so heavy that it pushed the land down in places. The lowland coastal areas of the Arctic Archipelago are a result of these glacial thrusts.

Ancient Animals of the North

Scientists studying the region have made some fascinating discoveries in recent years. They have found exotic animal and plant fossils in the North.

The fossils date back more than 3 million years. They include several species of animals that are now extinct, such as certain types of rabbits, beavers, and horses.

Scientists believe these animals once lived in a lush forest environment. This is very different from the barren tundra that covers much of the land today. It suggests the North was a much warmer region long ago. The average July temperature at that time might have been as much as 5° Celsius warmer than the current July average.

WHAT IS THE ARCTIC CORDILLERA?

The Arctic Cordillera is a vast mountain chain that runs through Ellesmere and Baffin Islands. This mountain chain includes parts of the North and Canadian Shield regions.

The mountains in this range include some of the tallest in Canada. In the northern part of the range, there are mountains over 2 kilometres tall. Ice caps cover these northern mountains. In the more humid southern end of the range, glaciers are common. The Arctic Cordillera is one of the main mountain chains in eastern Canada.

Animals and plants are scarce in this rugged, barren land. Bare rock dominates about three-quarters of the Arctic Cordillera, making it an inhospitable environment. Only about 1,000 people live in the Arctic Cordillera year-round. More than 80 percent of the population is Inuit.

The First Inhabitants

The first people to live on Canada's land were the indigenous peoples. According to the traditions of many indigenous peoples, they have lived on this land for as long as anyone can remember.

The Inuit

The first peoples to live in the North were the Inuit. Researchers have found evidence that the Inuit have lived in the region for more than 5,000 years.

Estimates of the Inuit population before European contact are unreliable, as the Inuit traditionally left few settlements behind them. As of 2001, there were over 45,000 Inuit living in Canada, many in the North.

Inuit hunters stand still while they wait for a seal to come up through the ice for air. Sometimes they have to stand perfectly still for hours while they wait.

" Researchers have found evidence that the Inuit have lived in the region for more than 5,000 years. "

Igloos are built in a spiral fashion from the inside. Furniture inside might include low platforms, cooking pots, and oil lamps.

Adapting to the Cold

The early inhabitants of the region had to be very resourceful and used their natural surroundings to help them survive the harsh winters found here.

The Inuit used snow and ice to create snowhouses called igloos. This is a special dwelling made out of blocks of ice. Temperatures inside an igloo are just below freezing or warmer.

Traditionally, the Inuit hunted local animals, such as walrus and whale. They used furs to make warm clothing, walrus tusks for spears for hunting, and animal fat to fuel oil lamps.

WHAT ARE INUIT COMMUNITIES LIKE TODAY?

Traditional activities, such as hunting, fishing, and trapping, continue to be an important part of the Inuit way of life. Modern technology is changing these traditional activities, however.

Today, wood-framed houses with oil-burning furnaces are more common than winter igloos. Modern technology has changed how the Inuit hunt. Hunters now use snowmobiles to journey across the vast northern lands rather than dogsleds. Also, rifles have replaced walrus tusks for hunting.

Arrivals from Europe

For early European explorers of the region, the North presented many opportunities and challenges. Over the last 500 years, people have come to the region searching for trade routes, hunting whales and Arctic fox, and, more recently, studying the frozen land of Canada's North.

The Search for the Northwest Passage

In the early 1500s, many Europeans journeyed the North's perilous lands hoping to find the **Northwest Passage.** The passage was an ideal trade route from North America to Asia. Well-known explorers such as John Cabot, Francis Drake, Martin Frobisher, Henry Hudson, and John Franklin braved the barren land. One by one they discovered the route was difficult to find, difficult to navigate, and often dangerous.

> **"** Maps were either incomplete or did not exist at all, so European explorers created their own with each new discovery. **"**

John Franklin, one of the best known explorers of the Canadian Arctic, used First Nations guides to help him explore the Arctic seaboard.

At the time, maps were either incomplete or did not exist at all. Explorers created their own maps with each new discovery. In 1906, Norwegian explorer Roald Amundsen was the first to navigate the Northwest Passage by sea.

Cultures Collide

Europeans brought new problems and opportunities to the Inuit. Europeans spread diseases, such as smallpox, tuberculosis, and influenza. They also introduced Inuit to new economic activities. The Inuit were eager to acquire European goods, such as guns, cloth, and beads, so they became fur trappers and helped the developing fur trade in Canada. The arrival of the Europeans changed the lives of the Inuit forever.

Roald Amundsen explored the Northwest Passage, the South Pole, and the North Pole.

QUICK FACTS

▸ The Northwest Passage extends about 1,450 kilometres from east to west.

▸ Entering the Northwest Passage from the Atlantic Ocean is extremely dangerous. There are about 50,000 icebergs. These icebergs can reach 90 metres in height, and are constantly drifting between Greenland and Baffin Island.

▸ Some claim that explorer Martin Frobisher created the first Thanksgiving in Newfoundland and Labrador in 1578 on his last attempt to find the Northwest Passage.

Tales from the North

LEGEND OF LUMAK

The Inuit of the North feel a special connection to the land. To them, there is a link between natural and supernatural worlds. The outcome of these tales taught children lessons of survival.

Lumak, a blind boy, lived with his mother and sister and their dog, Ukirk. One day, a polar bear appeared outside the window of the igloo. Lumak's mother handed the boy an arrow, led him to the window, and told him to kill the bear. Lumak shot the bear with an arrow. The mother turned to Lumak and said, "You killed Ukirk," but Lumak knew he had killed the bear.

The mother and sister left Lumak in the igloo and went to build a new igloo closer to where the bear had died. The mother sent the sister back with a bit of meat for Lumak, but told her to say that it was dog meat. When Lumak ate the meat, he knew it was polar bear meat, but he said nothing. As time passed, the old igloo began to collapse around Lumak where he sat alone and hungry.

One day a loon appeared and said to Lumak to come with him to the water. Once there, the loon told Lumak to hold onto him as he dove down into the water and not to move until he was out of air. Lumak did as the loon said. When they surfaced after a third time, Lumak regained his sight.

When Lumak returned to where his mother and sister lived, he pretended he was still blind. He asked his mother to help him catch a whale. When he got to the shore, Lumak prepared his harpoon and his line and told his mother to tie the line around her waist. She did as he asked. Finally, when Lumak saw a large whale, he shot his harpoon with all his might, but rather than help his mother, Lumak stood back and let the whale pull her into the sea.

NORTHERN LIGHTS AND HEAVY MISTS

The Inuit have traditional stories that explain how natural wonders were created. One of these stories is about the Northern Lights, and another is how the mists of spring first came to be.

Northern Lights

The Northern Lights are multi-coloured natural lights that appear in the sky. The Inuit describe the sky as a dome stretched over Earth. In the dome, there are many tiny holes that the spirits of the dead pass through to reach the heavenly regions.

The way to heaven passes over a narrow bridge that stretches across a deep gorge. The spirits already in heaven carry torches, which are the Northern Lights, to guide the new arrivals.

Heavy Mists

To explain why spring in the North is characterized by heavy mists, the Inuit speak of the great bullhead whale, the Creator's favourite animal. The Creator permitted man to hunt the bullhead for food but never for fun.

To help man hunt the whale, the Creator made spring. As the weather warmed, cracks appeared in the ice, letting the people get close enough to hunt the whale.

However, when the day came for the people to hunt the great bullhead whale, the Creator found he did not like to see the animal hunted. The Creator made spring mist to hide the whale from view.

Unique Islands

The Arctic Archipelago features more than twenty islands. There are a variety of landforms on the islands, including plains, fjords, and mountains.

Some of the World's Largest Islands

Ellesmere Island and Victoria Island are two of the largest islands in the world. Ellesmere Island covers 196,236 square kilometres of land, while Victoria Island covers 217,291 square kilometres. These two islands dominate much of the Canadian North.

Summers in the North are short and cool. On average, only 125 to 250 days each year reach a temperature over 5° Celsius.

Other large islands include King William Island and Banks Island. King William Island covers 13,111 square kilometres. Caribou and a small settlement of indigenous peoples inhabit the island. In 2001, King William Island had a population of 960.

Banks Island covers an area of more than 70,000 square kilometres. The only permanent settlement on the island is Sachs Harbour, which is on the southwesternmost coast. In 2001, the population of Banks Island was 114 people.

Desolate Devon Island

Devon Island is the largest uninhabited island on Earth. It covers an area of 55,000 square kilometres and is almost completely without life forms because of its northern latitude, high elevation, and bitterly cold temperatures. The island is home to a small population of musk-oxen and some small birds.

Devon Island was the site of a meteorite crash 23 million years ago. The meteorite left a 20-kilometre diameter crash impression that is now a lake. Scientists have learned that the crater's terrain has similarities to certain places on Mars.

QUICK FACTS

About 150,000 square kilometres of land on the Arctic islands are covered by glaciers.

The Arctic Archipelago is the world's second largest high-Arctic land area after Greenland.

Canadian **sovereignty** over the islands was not established until 1895.

Canada has 29 of the 100 largest islands in the world. This makes Canada the country with the greatest number of large islands.

Alert, a Canadian Forces Station located on the tip of Ellesmere Island, is the northernmost settlement in the world. It is only 834 kilometres from the North Pole.

Waters of the North

Aside from the wealth of islands in the North, the region includes significant bodies of water and waterway systems. North of the Arctic islands lies the Arctic Ocean, which is the smallest of the world's five oceans. Many **oceanography** experts consider the Arctic Ocean to be a sea rather than an ocean because of its small size.

The Amazing Arctic Ocean

The Arctic Ocean covers an area of over 14 million square kilometres. It borders 45,389 kilometres of coastline and is nearly completely landlocked by the many surrounding landmasses. Smaller bodies of water and waterways are found within the Arctic Ocean. These include Baffin Bay, Beaufort Sea, Greenland Sea, Hudson Bay, Hudson Strait, and the White Sea. The Arctic Ocean links with the Pacific Ocean by the Bering Strait, and connects to the Atlantic Ocean by way of the Greenland Sea.

> **"** The floor of the Arctic Ocean consists mainly of basins, deeps, and abysses. **"**

The floor of the Arctic Ocean consists mainly of basins, deeps, and **abysses**. On average, the ocean's depth is about 1,300 metres. In winter, it is covered by a permanent cap of sea ice. In summer, open water can be found along the coasts.

Approximately 20 percent of an iceberg is visible above water. The other 80 percent is underwater.

While the Arctic Ocean borders on some of the most desolate and uninhabited land on the planet, it boasts at least ten ports and harbours. In recent years, the Arctic Ocean has become important to commercial enterprises that seek to use the seasonal Northwest Passage waterway.

Beaufort Sea

The Beaufort Sea borders the Arctic Archipelago to the west. This body of water is rich in petroleum and covers an area of over 450,000 square kilometres. The Mackenzie River system is a waterway with smaller rivers that empty directly into the Beaufort Sea. This waterway is inhabited by many Arctic species, including whales and various sea birds.

Axel Heiberg Island in Canada's remote North is surrounded by moving sea ice for most of the year.

WHAT LANDFORMS ARE FOUND IN THE NORTH?

The North consists of many landforms, such as pingos, glacial cirques, and tors, that are not found in more temperate climates.

Pingos are cone-shaped hills that have a core of clear ice. Some pingos stretch as high as 90 metres. On the flat delta, pingos are landmarks.

Glacial cirques are rounded, bowl-shaped depressions that are partially surrounded by steep cliffs. They are formed by glacial erosion. The highest cliff is often called a "headwall."

Tors are tower-like features that stand above a smooth surface. They are formed by a long period of **weathering**.

The Northern Climate

The climate of the North presents many challenges for life in the region. The subzero temperatures freeze exposed skin, turn moisture from exhaled air into ice, and create an uninhabitable environment.

Ice and Glaciers

The North's low temperatures have a profound impact on the land, air, and water in the region. The waters are almost always frozen, or littered with massive chunks of ice.

> **"** The cold temperatures feel even colder when there is a strong wind. **"**

Glaciers are one of the North's most recognizable features. While the eastern islands of the Arctic Archipelago contain many mountain glaciers, the western islands contain almost none. Many glaciers are less than 1 kilometre long, but some glaciers extend more than 100 kilometres in length.

Ice floes are floating chunks of sea ice that are less than 10 kilometres in diameter.

Lichens are the main food source for reindeer and caribou. Toxic substances from pollution can contaminate lichens, which can harm the animals that feed on them.

Effects of the Cold

The North's temperature is so cold that most of the land is permanently frozen, creating **permafrost**. These conditions make it very difficult for vegetation to grow.

For humans and wildlife in the region, the cold temperatures feel even colder when there is a strong wind. This "wind chill" effect causes temperatures to feel even lower than they are. When winds are high and temperatures are low, people and animals are at a higher risk of frostbite and **hypothermia**.

QUICK FACTS

- In February of 1979, temperatures in Iqaluit reached lows of –40° Celsius, with winds of 100 kilometres per hour. These conditions led to zero visibility in snow, which kept residents indoors for 10 days.

- Glaciers and ice fields cover approximately 200,000 square kilometres, or 2 percent of Canada's total area.

- The only glaciers on the western islands of the Arctic Archipelago are on Melville Island.

- Due to **global warming**, average Arctic summer temperatures have risen by about 1.2° Celsius per decade since the 1980s.

Charting the Climate

A region's climate can indicate what it is like to live there. Temperature, snowfall, and even growing seasons are all part of climate.

Information is collected when studying a region's climate. The maps and charts on these pages help describe this information in a visual way.

Average Temperature

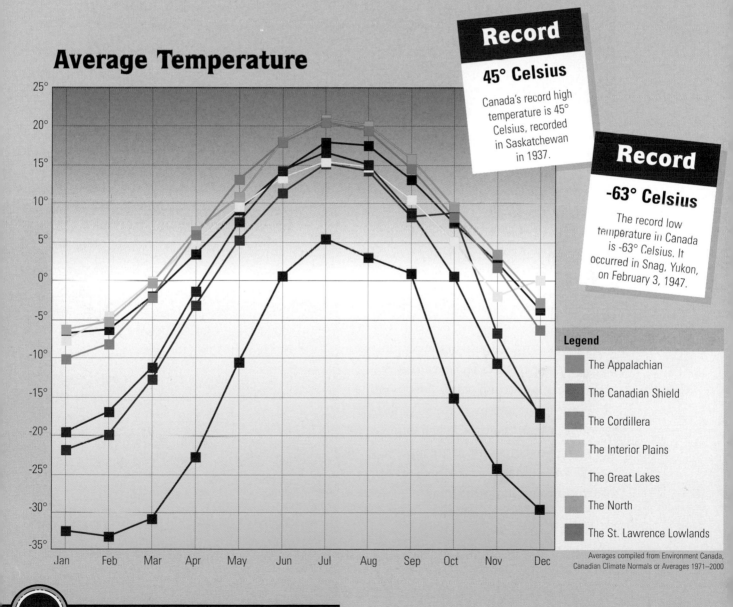

Record

45° Celsius

Canada's record high temperature is 45° Celsius, recorded in Saskatchewan in 1937.

Record

-63° Celsius

The record low temperature in Canada is -63° Celsius. It occurred in Snag, Yukon, on February 3, 1947.

Legend

- The Appalachian
- The Canadian Shield
- The Cordillera
- The Interior Plains
- The Great Lakes
- The North
- The St. Lawrence Lowlands

Averages compiled from Environment Canada, Canadian Climate Normals or Averages 1971–2000

Average Snowfall

Legend

■	over 400 cm
■	300 - 400 cm
■	200 - 300 cm
■	100 - 200 cm
■	under 100 cm

Source: Canadian Oxford World Atlas, 4th Edition, 1998

Record

118.1 cm

The record 1-day snowfall, on January 17, 1974, was 118.1 centimetres at Lakelse Lake, British Columbia.

Growing Season

Legend

Average number of days with a median temperature over 5° C

■	under 60
■	60 - 100
■	100 - 140
■	140 - 180
■	180 - 220
■	220 - 260
■	over 260

Source: Canadian Oxford World Atlas, 4th Edition, 1998

Rising Temperatures, Rising Waters

Although freezing temperatures are common in the North, average temperatures are beginning to rise. Some scientists predict winter temperatures in the region to rise by 5° to 10° Celsius during the next century.

Rising surface temperatures are slowly altering the North's natural environment. The thickness of the polar ice is decreasing, which is causing water levels to rise. Over time, rising water levels may lead to extreme flooding. This alarming trend has scientists worried because the effects of global warming are becoming visible throughout the region.

" The effects of global warming are becoming visible throughout the North. "

Musk-oxen have longer hair than any other animal in North America, keeping them insulated against the frigid Arctic air.

Effect on the Food Chain

All of the North's animals are connected to the **food chain**. The slightest changes at the bottom of the food chain affect other animals in the same chain. An example has been noted in the spring when a certain type of **phytoplankton** blooms. It is declining because water temperatures are rising. This means that zooplankton that feed on the phytoplankton are declining as well. As a result of fewer zooplankton, there is less food for the fish larvae that feed on them. Less food for the fish that eat the fish larvae means less food for the birds that eat fish.

Effect on Humans

The impact of global warming on humans is subtle. Some Inuit communities are reporting problems unfamiliar to them, such as sunburns from increased sunlight and allergies caused by the effects of increased plant growth. As global warming increases, changes in the food chain will also affect the Inuit, who rely on animals for food.

Industry will also experience changes as a result of global warming. Today, buildings have been constructed on the permafrost. As the permafrost continues to thaw, pipelines, airports, and roads may soon slide into bogs or marshes.

CAN GLOBAL WARMING HELP THE PEOPLE OF THE NORTH?

Global warming affects climate, vegetation, wildlife, and people. While many problems stem from global warming, this climate change could provide advantages for the North region.

The rising temperatures, which lead to the melting of ice-clogged waterways, could lead to easier mining and transportation. The Northwest Passage would become a year-round route, and the area would also see a dramatic increase in development due to the easier access to resources.

Untapped Natural Resources

C anada's North is the world's greatest area of untapped resources. However, conditions in the region make these resources difficult to find and extract.

Renewable Resources

Renewable resources are resources that are replaced naturally over time, such as plant and animal life. As the North has little vegetation that is suitable for agriculture and no trees to support a lumber industry, its main renewable resources are its animals. The region has an abundance of fish and other wildlife that can be used for meat and fur. There is also a great number of fishery opportunities in the area.

Non-Renewable Resources

Non-renewable resources are substances that cannot grow back naturally when taken from an area. The non-renewable resources found in the North include metals and minerals, such as lead, zinc, tungsten, lithium, uranium, iron ore, copper, nickel,

Arctic char live farther north than any other freshwater fish.

Icebreakers have powerful engines that propel the ship up and forward, crashing down on the ice below.

diamonds, gold, silver, and platinum. Coal and oil are also found in the region.

Natural resources in the North are difficult to reach. Drilling for oil and other resources requires advanced technology that is expensive and difficult to transport.

Freshwater Supplies

The North's fresh water is one of the few freshwater supplies in the world that have not been heavily spoiled by pollution. Abundant fresh water locked inside glaciers is a key resource in the region as pure water remains preserved for longer periods of time.

WHAT ARE ICEBREAKERS?

Icebreakers are key to transporting important resources, such as oil and gas, from the frozen region.

Icebreakers are ships that are designed to break up ice-covered waters. They are often used to clear a path for government supply and development operations in the North. Icebreakers have been used in the region since the 1920s.

Canada has 21 of the 110 icebreakers used around the world. Canada's fleet of icebreakers is expected to become larger and more advanced in the near future.

Soil Quality

The quality of the soil in the North is quite poor for growing crops. Factors that play a role in the region's soil quality include the cold climate and low precipitation.

Frozen Ground

When discussing the soil quality in the North, climate is an important issue. Year-round cold temperatures permanantly freeze the ground, creating permafrost.

66 Permafrost can reach as deep as 1,000 metres into the soil of the high Arctic islands. **99**

Permafrost is a rock-hard mixture of ice, stone, and soil that water and vegetation cannot penetrate. The coldest ground temperatures in permafrost worldwide are found on Ellesmere Island. There, the ground temperature sits at about −15° Celsius.

The islands and mainland in the North comprise a series of rolling hills and plains. Lakes and ponds make up less than 1 percent of the region.

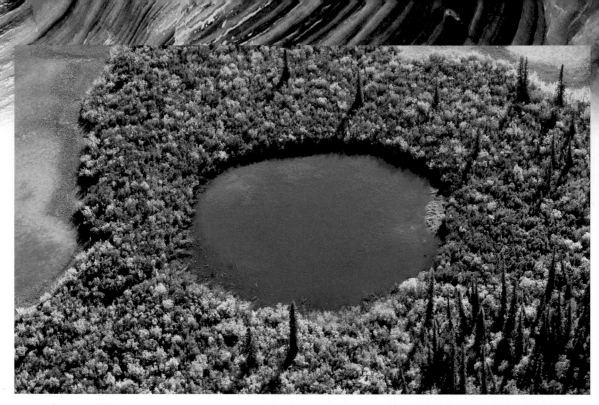

Many plants in the Arctic are very small because their roots grow in the thin, unfrozen layer of soil above the permafrost.

Permafrost can reach as deep as 1,000 metres into the soil of the islands in the region. Subzero soil temperatures minimize the growth and activity of microorganisms that provide essential nutrients needed for vegetation growth. As a result, most plant life in the region is small and close to the ground.

As well, organic matter in the soil tends to decompose very slowly because of subzero temperatures. This makes the soil even less nutritious for vegetation.

Precipitation

The North receives very little precipitation year-round. Average annual precipitation ranges from 1 to 5 centimetres. This lack of moisture results in polar desert soils, which dominate the region. Only a few plants, such as sedges and mosses, can grow in areas with such low precipitation.

QUICK FACTS

- The slow decay of plant life in the Arctic is helpful. The Arctic stores nearly one-third of Earth's carbon. As the permafrost thaws from global warming, the vegetation will also decay more quickly. This will increase the amount of carbon dioxide in the atmosphere and speed up global warming.

- There are no earthworms in the Arctic. Earthworms help break down decaying matter in the soil.

- Scientists predict that global warming could eventually increase precipitation in the North by as much as 25 percent.

Growing Things

Even with its poor growing conditions, the North does have some vegetation. The few plants, trees, and shrubs that grow within the region show that plant growth can occur in cold regions.

Plants and Ferns

There are about 300 known plants and ferns that grow in the North during certain seasons. These plants include moss, purple saxifrage, dwarf birch, grass, lichen, Arctic cotton, and sedges.

Much of the vegetation in the North grows low to the ground and tends to be small. Even these few plants and ferns are quite rare in the most northern portion of the North, where the land is dominated by polar deserts.

> " There are about 300 known plants and ferns that grow in the North during certain seasons. "

Lichens reproduce by having portions break off and fall away to begin new growth.

Fruits such as berries and sorrel are important to the people living in the region. Berries, including wild blueberries and bearberries, are harvested throughout the summer. Some species of mountain sorrel, such as rhubarb and buckwheat, are sources of food, and a few species are grown as ornamentals.

Trees in the North

Tree growth in the North is extremely slow. Still, some species of willow trees can be found in the area. The dwarf willow, one of the only wood species in the region, grows in dense, twisted ground along some parts of Melville Island. The willows lie flat to the ground, which protects them from the harsh winds.

Single-celled Plants

While permafrost makes most plant growth difficult, it can help the growth of some vegetation.

In summer, the topsoil thaws slightly, which allows for a small layer of vegetation to grow. This includes the single-celled plants known as phytoplankton. These plants can even bloom under thin ice.

Due to the short growing season, northern wildflowers bloom for only a short period during the year.

WHAT IS THE ARCTIC POPPY?

A particularly well-adapted plant found throughout the region is the Arctic poppy. Its shape, heat-absorbing centre, and ability to track the Sun's movement through the sky make it a natural solar collector. This rise in its internal temperature slows the formation and ripening of seeds. Reproduction is then promoted by attracting **pollinating** insects that come to bask in the flower's warmth.

Wildlife of the North

A variety of different animals, fish, and birds live in the North. In the past, the North was the site of an important fur-trading operation for the Arctic fox. Its waters were also heavily hunted for whales. These operations in the North had a tremendous impact on the wildlife living there.

Animals of the North

The animals that live in the area have a thick layer of fat that protects them from the harsh northern climate. Some animals in the region include polar bears, reindeer, moose, wolves, ground squirrels, weasels, and shaggy musk-ox. In 2003, a grizzly bear's tracks were found in the region, making it the northernmost location ever to have been visited by a grizzly.

> " The region may even house marine creatures that have yet to be identified. "

Polar bears remain active during the winter, unlike other species of bears that sleep for most of the season. They hunt and travel on sea ice, waiting beside breathing holes to capture seals.

Birds of the North

Many different birds travel to and from the North. Almost seventy-five different bird species **migrate** to the area in the short summer season. Birds that stay year-round include ravens, owls, gulls, and ptarmigans. Other birds found in the region include the snow bunting, peregrine falcon, Arctic tern, snow goose, and the gyrfalcon.

Fish of the North

The marine wildlife and fish populations of the North are migratory. Marine mammals include beluga whales, seals, walruses, and narwhals. Approximately seventy different species of fish, including Arctic char, whitefish, and pike, are found in many bodies of water in the North. The bowhead whale is the largest animal in the Arctic Ocean. It is an endangered species.

The region may even house marine creatures that have yet to be identified. Some scientists are hoping to discover hundreds of new and undiscovered animals and marine wildlife in the vast North.

White-tailed ptarmigans have fully-feathered feet. They act as snowshoes, allowing the birds to walk on snow while insulating their feet against the cold.

WHAT IS THE THICK-BILLED MURRE?

The thick-billed murre is a summer visitor to the North. Large numbers of these birds roost on the rocky ledges of the islands in the Arctic Archipelago.

The thick-billed murre has short, stubby wings that make flying difficult. These birds migrate to Newfoundland every winter by swimming. They use their short wings as propellers when they dive underwater for fish to eat.

The thick-billed murre lays a single egg in the breeding season. Both parents share the responsibility of feeding the chick in the nest.

A Fragile Environment

The Canadian North has a fragile environment. Global warming and increasing pollution are just two of the threats facing the region.

A Warmer North

Global warming has a profound impact on the food chain in the North. Cotton grass, an important food source for migrating caribou, now blooms earlier than usual on the tundra because of the warmer winters. Caribou miss the cotton grass bloom because they arrive too late to feed on it. They must search for other food sources.

> " Even radioactive substances have found their way to the remote North. "

Pipelines transport enormous quantities of petroleum, gasoline, chemicals, and other products long distances. Pipeline companies based in Calgary and Vancouver transport petroleum in Canada.

Pollution Problems

Global warming is not the only threat to the food chain in the North. Man-made pollutants are becoming an increasing problem as more human development occurs in the region. Some toxic chemicals present a problem because they stay in the environment for years. They are digested by animals, which are then eaten by the Inuit. These toxic pollutants can have dangerous effects on animals' and peoples' health.

Pollution from man-made chemicals and substances also affect the global atmophere. Air pollution from industries in other regions find their way into the atmosphere. Pollutants are absorbed into water vapour, blown by strong winds, and fall to Earth in the form of acid rain, harming plant and animal life in the region. As well, **greenhouse gases** trap heat in the atmosphere and contribute to global warming.

Even radioactive substances have found their way to the remote North. **Radionuclides**, from the 1986 Chernobyl nuclear plant explosion in the former Soviet Union and other man-made sources, drifted into Canada's North. Scientists believe these substances can cause cancer.

Q Should shipping traffic and oil drilling be permitted in the North region?	
NO	**YES**
If a disaster occurs in the remote region, it will take a long time to send help to the affected area.	Ships are needed to bring supplies to Arctic settlements.
Oil and pollution have a negative effect on wildlife, either through hypothermia or poisoning.	Drilling for oil will provide more jobs and benefit Canada's economy.
Oil remains toxic longer in cold waters, compared to warmer waters. It would be much more difficult to clean up a spill in frigid Arctic water.	More shipping routes through the North will increase Canadian and global trade.

View from Above

There are different ways to view a region. Maps and photos, including those from satellites, help to show the region in different ways.

A map is a diagram that shows an area's surface. Maps can demonstrate many details, such as lakes, rivers, borders, towns, and even roads.

Photos can demonstrate what a region looks like close up. In a photo, specific objects, such as buildings, people, and animals, can be seen.

Satellite photos are pictures taken from space. A satellite thousands of metres in the air can show details as small as a car.

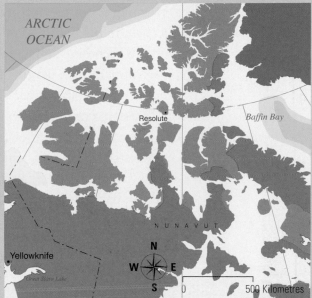

Questions:

What kind of information can be learned from a photo?

How might a map be useful?

What details can be seen on a satellite photo that cannot be seen on a map?

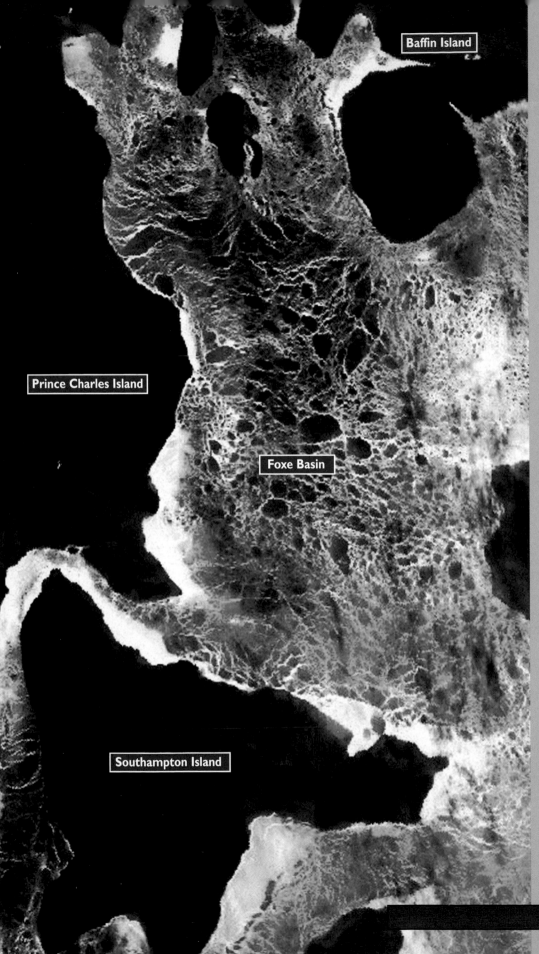

Baffin Island

Prince Charles Island

Foxe Basin

Southampton Island

Satellite Image of Foxe Basin

Foxe Basin is a waterway between Baffin Island and the Melville Peninsula. The basin is a shallow depression and is rarely free of ice year-round. Landfast ice, or sea ice attached to the coast, dominates the northern part of the Basin. Pack ice, or sea ice other than landfast ice, covers the deeper southern waters.

Nighttime **thermal imaging** shows ice covering the Foxe Basin in whitish-blue colour, and snow-covered land appears deep blue or dark in colour.

Although Foxe Basin is a little known area, it is one of the most biologically rich and diverse waterways in the Canadian North.

What do you notice about this satellite photo compared to a regular photo? What information can you learn from it that you would not learn from a map?

Technology Tools

People have studied geology for hundreds of years. Geologists study the rocks, earth, and surfaces that make up Earth. Even before the science of geology had a name, ancient peoples studied the rocks and minerals around them. They experimented to find out what kind of rocks were used to make weapons, jewellery, and items they needed in daily life. Flint, a type of rock that is easy to shape and sharpen, was used to make spears. Minerals, such as gold and copper, were too soft to use as weapons or tools and were shaped to make beautiful jewellery.

Today, geologists use some tools that have been around for centuries, as well as more modern tools. These tools range from simple pick hammers to sophisticated computer equipment. Geologists use these tools to study the rocks and minerals they find on land. They study geology in other areas, as well. Modern technology and tools help them study geology under the sea, in volcanoes, and even on the Moon.

Careers in Geology

What does a geophysicist do?

Answer: A geophysicist uses gravity, as well as magnetic, seismic, and electrical methods to study the earth, to find resources, and to help plan development. A geophysicist can work outside in the field, or indoors, using computers for models and calculations.

Tools of the Trade

Rock hammer or pick:
These special hammers have a flat end that is used to crush larger pieces of rock, and a pointed end, which is used to pick away smaller pieces of rock.

X rays:
X rays help geologists study material in detail. Certain crystals or minerals can be examined very closely by an X ray. Geologists studying ancient fossils or artifacts also use X rays so they can examine delicate objects without damaging them.

Compass:
A compass helps geologists tell which direction they are going. Compasses are very important to geologists, who often work from maps to travel to the areas they are studying.

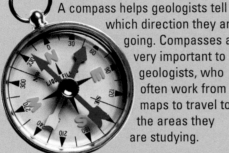

Seismograph:
A seismograph measures Earth's vibrations. Geologists use seismographs to study the movements of Earth's tectonic plates. Tectonic plates are huge slabs of rock that shift and move beneath Earth's surface. When two or more plates collide, there is an earthquake.

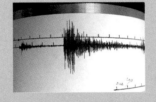

Brushes:
Some of the rocks and materials geologists study are very delicate. Once geologists have uncovered an object in the rock or soil, they use soft brushes to remove dust and debris without causing damage.

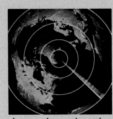

Sonar:
Sonar helps geologists map areas that cannot be reached by humans or seen by the human eye. Sonar sends out a beam of sound. Geologists determine what the sonar has hit by the type of vibration that returns. They can map these locations by listening to the sound.

What is a climatologist?

Answer: A climatologist studies climate and weather patterns. Climatologists research weather patterns to predict what the weather will be like in the future, and how the weather might affect the land. They analyze and interpret maps, photographs, and charts to draw conclusions.

Mapping a Route

One of the greatest challenges for early explorers of the North was the lack of accurate, detailed maps. As they navigated their way through unfamiliar territory, they created maps to show where they went and what they observed. Those who followed them used these maps to find their way.

Imagine you are one of the early explorers. Your task is to create a map of an area in your community so that someone else can follow the route you took to arrive at a chosen spot. The area that you choose will be "new land."

1. Choose an interesting route, with unexpected twists and turns, in your community.

2. As you walk along the route, sketch on a piece of paper what you observe on both sides of your path.

3. When you return home, organize your sketch into a map. Use symbols on your map to represent what you saw. Take care to show exactly where each landmark is in relation to other objects. Use a key to explain each symbol. Include a compass rose. Remember that north always points to the top of a map.

4. The true test of your map will be to ask your friend or neighbour to use your map to follow the same route as you. Using the information on your map, can they arrive at the same spot that you did?

Navigating to the North Pole

Imagine you are an explorer in the early 1900s before the North Pole was discovered. Your task is to plan a trip to the North Pole.

You will begin your journey from the capital city of the Yukon Territory, the Northwest Territories, or Nunavut. Which route will you take from your chosen capital city to the North Pole?

1. At which capital city will you begin your journey?

2. What supplies will you take with you?

3. How will you get your crew and supplies to your starting point?

4. What forms of transportation will you use to reach the North Pole?

5. In which season will you travel?

6. Which waterways will you use?

7. Which islands will you cross to reach the North Pole?

8. Where will you and your crew rest?

On a map of Canada's North, show the route you will take to reach the North Pole. Show where you will stop to rest and how far you hope to travel between resting points. When others look at your map, they should be able to see exactly where you will go and how far you hope to travel each day of your journey.

Further Research

Books

Find out more about the North.

Miller, Debbie. *Arctic Lights, Arctic Nights*. New York, NY: Walker and Company, 2003.

Rau, Dana Meachen. *Arctic Adventure: Inuit Life in the 1800s*. Norwalk, CT: Soundprints, 2003.

Web Sites

To learn more about the North region, visit:

The Canadian Encyclopedia
www.thecanadianencyclopedia.com

To find more maps and photos of the North, visit:

Canadian Geographic
www.canadiangeographic.ca/

Glossary

abysses: the deepest parts of the ocean

archipelago: a chain or cluster of islands

biome: the habitat found on Earth, organized according to the predominant vegetation

continental drift: the theory that Earth was once made up of one supercontinent that broke up, becoming today's seven continents

food chain: a series of organisms in an ecological community

global warming: an increase in the average temperature of Earth's atmosphere, enough to cause climate change

greenhouse gases: atmospheric gases that can reflect heat back to Earth

hypothermia: lower than normal body temperature

Ice Age: a period of extremely low temperatures across Earth, accompanied by a growth of polar ice sheets

migrate: to travel from one region of Earth to another, usually on a seasonal basis

Northwest Passage: an Arctic shipping route that links the Atlantic and Pacific Oceans

oceanography: the science that studies oceans and ocean life

permafrost: ground or subsoil that is permanently frozen

phytoplankton: microscopic plants

pollinating: fertilizing by transferring pollen

radionuclides: atoms with an unstable nucleus that give off radiation

solstice: when the Sun is at its greatest distance from the equator; occurs twice a year

sovereignty: power or authority over

thermal imaging: infrared channels measuring land and sea surface temperatures

tundra: a barren, treeless plain

weathering: the effects of air, water, or frost on rocks

Index